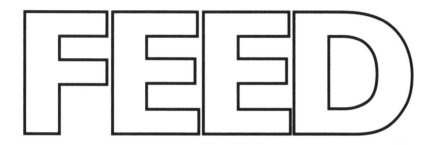

Published by Tin House Books, Portland, Oregon

Distributed by W. W. Norton & Company

Library of Congress Cataloging-in-Publication Data

Names: Pico, Tommy, author.
Title: Feed / Tommy Pico.
Description: First U.S. edition. | Portland, OR : Tin House Books, 2019.
Identifiers: LCCN 2019013806| ISBN 9781947793576 (paperback) |
  ISBN 9781947793583 (ebook)
Classification: LCC PS3616.I288 F44 2019 | DDC 811/.6—dc23
LC record available at https://lccn.loc.gov/2019013806

First U.S. Edition 2019
Printed in the USA
Interior design by Jakob Vala

www.tinhouse.com

FEED

TOMMY PICO

TIN HOUSE BOOKS / Portland, Oregon

Me n Leo yakkity yak yak'd
about writer's
block
and the starchy long stroke of quote unquote God on the Meadow Walk
and he didn't know I was fully head over banana peels I mean in Kiehl's
I mean in straight up crappy love with him yet and maybe I didn't
either? Sand crabs poking their bodies & legs post wave Hindsight

is Good & Plenty I mean 20/20
clearly
the worst American
candy And what is candy, but a crush?

Leo said it's tangled up
in waves in dreams in therapy That writer's block
(or is it god?)
comes from being blocked up
in other parts of the days
of our lives
of our lives
of our lives

This is a polysaccharide Effective deflection
Rejection heavy,
that he'd forgotten what the feeling
of a good
idea is

But I'm standing right in front of you?

I thought bubbled but never troubled
the air
with my utterance
Instead I said, "this is the part where you ask me for my number"

because I was committed
to being my own damn romantic
comedy that year—

Our sublime times The Don Julio margarita mix of our situationship

These are the Doppler blips
that ripple resurface
when Leo surfaces among the Chelsea Thicket
Optimal frustration from the Odysseus years Golden Fleece of
intimacy
for the first time in like what
6 months?
A year?
Two years?
Seven years?
Has it been SEVEN years? 1492? It was literally 69 billion years BC

Dear reader,

White as a bell you whisk me to a fever
like the ruby cinnamon—Hey! Let's make a vinaigrette

Did you know molasses emulsifies the olive
oil and keeps the little
fat
molecules from stumbling
into each other, thus allowing the oil and vinegar
to mix?

A sauce is broken when the oil separates

like a heart

Sometimes this is inevitable, no matter how hard you shake the mason jar

A bumble bee's tiny hairs curl

THE EPA'S PLAN TO CENSOR CLIMATE CHANGE DATA

in the electric field
of a flower
and the seasons and the fields sway
their harvest like a rolling
sea

The city cabin-fevered in the wake of winter, Sherlock & looking glass
(it's a gas, gas, gas)'d for an excuse
to wear an eyebrow lift of shorts again
I don't know what this flower
is called
but in the breeze
it looks like a butterfly on a string The dependably wild
inconsistencies of spring Now the city
keeps a sweater in its backpack—Balance

is not unlike how rice and beans shouted "You complete me!" in the
crowded train station millions of years ago. Dice the leeks. Snap off

the inedible ends of the asparagus

Salt/salt/salt until you can angel in it

Wilkes: How do you feel?
She swipes a curl from her face, blows out a swirl of smoke and bangs
ashes into my baby cactus
Me: Like someone put a sleeve of dry pasta up a mouse's urethra?

She didn't ash into my baby cactus. I just like the way that sounds. We're on her fire escape overlooking the belly garden of all Brooklyn apartment buildings. The day was in the low 60s but we're in the high weeds. She ashes between the irons. Her landlord is back there, pulling plants and sucking her teeth.

Wilkes: ASH HAPPENS!

she shouts down. The landlord shakes her head, says something low and out of range.

Wilkes: I mean about seeing Leo again

Me: Everyone is talking about the Fermi Paradox right now, you know what that is?

She hands me the spliff. I hold it eye level, staring at the ember raveling the white paper black and grey before crumbling away

Wilkes: Of *course*! I wrote the book on Farm Socks!

She rolls her eyes and lifts her palms up.

Me: It's like, against the infinity of space and all those stars and all those worlds out there, the probability of extraterrestrial civilizations other than us is extremely high. But where are they? Even if interstellar travel is really slow, our sun is relatively young compared to the age of the universe as a whole. They'd have had millions of years to get here.

Wilkes: I think it's paternalistic to assume we'd be demonstrably visited in our lifetimes. History basically *just* started recording itself. They could have come a million years ago and been like, this rock is trash! If . . . you're not gonna smoke that? Pass, plz

Nations are always outlived by their cities

Dear reader,

We are in a pot.

One of us is the vegetables and one of us is the water. I can't tell
who is cooking who, like a late 80s Aretha Franklin song—we give
ourselves up to each other. Into each other. Throughout each other. I
THINK whoops I think *that* exchange is what Beyoncé
bards about in "XO," her love song to the crowd

Track 1: "XO" by Beyoncé. The part where she looks out into the
crowd and assures them, *they* are what she needs. That she gives them
everything. It doesn't deny finality. Love, then lights out. It simply
identifies the grain of performance is her feed.

I'm going to keep this short
and sweet bc I am tall and BITTER:

There's a kind of stability
There's a kind of stability
There's a kind of stability
being so thoroughly Teebs I mean seen
A sly calm, indulging the part of you that stays when the rest hides
or hurricanes away onstage. Another tug of skin on my skin, firming
everything in place

Dr. John says *anxiety of the return is necessary. Conclusion*
must come for a new story
to take place

Track 2: "We Need a Resolution" by Aaliyah. The part where you
reach the critical juncture of whether the relationship can be
salvaged. Do I change? Do you change? Do we go on the same?
Hurt is inescapable here. This resolve dissolves the doubt: We need
to talk it out. Evasion writ large: The reason why we don't have the
conversation is because we're afraid we already know the answer.

Dear reader,

I've been thinking about fuel sources that produce the heat of the
fire that burns inside you and the term "resistive circuit" and active
networks and mainly about Kirchhoff's current law, that the sum of all
currents entering a node is equal to the sum of all currents leaving the
node by which I mean it's pollen season again and it's got my circuitry
inconsolable and the City stopped texting me back which, wtf I've
never been ghosted on by a whole City It's very *men* TFW you want
the City to know you hate it, but also like it doesn't even occur to you
to think about the City—Wait who are you? Ooh yeah, yr whatever
anyway I'm having the Baja fish tacos you shd go to shell Sorry I mean
have the macaroni I hear it's Wait a minute who are you again? I'm
talking to the freaking reader can you give me a minute jfc
I've been thinking
a lot about stretch denim
that doesn't also have a stretchy waistband
(by which I mean nature's cruelest disagreements)
and I've been thinking
about the slobbering of heat that is the promise of spring.

In her book *An Everlasting Meal* Tamar Adler,
waxing poetic on boiling cauliflower,
writes, "Heat is a vital broker between separate things."

In the insanely popular early 90s alternative rock banger "Linger,"
Dolores O'Riordan sings, "If you
if you could return:
don't let it burn.
Don't let it fade."

Today, to wear out the woozy, to giddy the skittish dizzy into a steady
simple rush of stillness I buttered

around the city listening to The Cranberries
as the air around me bounded
into its summer self
but literally two weeks ago there was a blizzard
that thawed into a song.

Springtime is so insecure, right?
But at least we know where it's heading Fiery
lion I lay no claim on but whatever memory lies all the time

[in three voices, like a braid: Gansevoort Woodland]
Appalachian red, Cercis canadensis; SER-sis kan-uh-DEN-sis
gray birches, Betula populifolia; BET-yoo-luh pop-yoo-lih-FOLE-ee-uh
dogwoods, Cornus florida

Are you an introvert or an extrovert? he whispers blacklight
blackout
as his bitty big balls bounce
against the throat
of my taint

(by which I just mean my taint)

Dear reader,
I am a hoar on a book tour and traveling
is so romantic, ain't it? An ode

that bodes of dynamism
and gutter sluttery. Glittering sea
of one night stand and
kick
stand

dicks
Camel Blue ash and pit stain tees

ALEXA–SIRI:

(What time does Panda Express open?)

Panda Express, I mean James Brown, is dead

Crowbar kraken awake every fire hydrant
on every corner
of every city
block

and mainline that shit into my veins.

I'm planted
in mustard-yellow slip
ons at the waterfront
of a new city made of mustard
greens, metaphorical tether ball water features

and a literal city.

SEPTA. Charm City Circulator. MBTA.

I'm sprouting
a pink tank
top
at the bus stop of a new city
made of absinthe bird
sanctuaries, metaphorical troll doll jewel belly

t-shirts
and literal

britches.

I mean bridges.

El train. Amtrak. Trolley.

I've grown
spray-on skinny
high waisted acid washed old-fashioneds
at the hotel bar
in a new city
made of tucked in black *Wayne's World* t-shirts
(oh dream weaver)

and literal roundabouts.

the MARTA. the Marc. the MAX.

Track 3: "Alone" by Heart. The part where she expresses doubt about
being able to confess her feelings to the lover, and wonders at what
point she'll be able to get the lover away from all others, "Alone," in
order to unload.

Portland Oregon is a bunch of white ppl in a brew pub whose name is
two random nouns like Sage & Mortar or Whimsy + Pickles or Straw
and Freddy Krueger Glove Expectant
faces expecting
me
to smile back. I don't do that.

Portland Maine, the other white Portland, is a bunch of full leg pants
and poly pan-
sexuals

Tonight I am pierogies
Ross Pierogies
Beer battered fish tacos and jalapeño corn
bread Aloe lavender under-eye nipple goops
Obsessively checking my bank balance
and vocal rest
stop
in Connecticut
that has a Sbarro, a pick n mix candy store, a Taco Bell *AND* Chipotle:
Proof that linear time is a gd sham

Once, I wrote about being ancestrally from a desert
that drought made me restless
searching for a nourishing territory
You know how some people
are "all that"? Well I'm all appetite Hunger pang
an ambulance
siren speeding to another needy feeling
The vernal bend rendering the cell walls softer, pliable without fully
spilling into each other

Shall I be a poem for you?
I mean, I used "shall" tbh
me af
the human condition smdh
the bible lol
bibliosexual wtf
the library iykwim
No territory will ever satisfy me

af

SAVE OUR COURTS! SIGN THIS PETITION!

Dear reader,

A roux, I've learned tonight in this midcity dinner party apartment tucked somewhat safely away from asthmatic LA freeways, is the mixture of butter and flour used to swell sauces and soups and Paul's baked sage mac n cheese that I'm whisking alive like an al dente Evanescence cheese-rock bop. Whistle while you whisk away the rage scrunched in yr boulders. I says to them around the table I says—

I don't have a food history.

If the dish is, "subjugate an indigenous population," here's an ingredient of the roux: alienate us from our traditional ways of gathering and cooking food.

Kumeyaays moved around what wd be called San Diego County with the seasons. The mountains, the valleys, the coast. Not much arable land or big game so we followed the food wherever it would go.

Then the missions. Then isolated reservations on stone mountains where not even a goat could live. Then the starvation. Then the Food Distribution Program on Indian Reservations. Whatever the military would throw away came canned in the backs of trucks. The commodities. The powdered milk, worms in the oatmeal, corn syrupy canned peaches. Food stripped of its nutrients. Then came the sugar blood. The sickness. The glucose meter goes up and up and up.

I says to them around the table I says, I don't have food stories. With you, I say, I'm cooking new ones.

Being protective
of yr recipes is only natural. Things get stolen.

Cousin dies, some overdose, and another cousin
has a daughter Incel man
plows
into ppl w/ a truck in Toronto mostly women
and there r something like 70 million
more men than women in China & India and

Roy SAYS HE HAS whoops says he has
a new metaphor, except it's not
a metaphor A literal part of his
heart
has died
says the echocardiogram
he got before starting a new med
but it's fine he just needs to eat more farty
salads and "Mamihlapinatapai" is the most precise
word according to linguists
from the Yaghan language of Tierra del Fuego
something like when you leave a café bathroom and want to tell the
next person in line it wasn't you who took the smelliest dump in
American history but you keep walking I mean
the word is more like when two ppl look
at each other and the look
is that they both
know

what the other shd do but neither
wants to initiate How in Kumeyaay, "howka" means "hello" but more
like *I see the fire that burns inside you* A whole caravan of meaning in a
single word and Wilkes

after twalkin bout her non-invasive surgery
says John Krasinski, at 6'3, is the *shortest* of three
brothers the others 6'8 and 6'9 and I start to
pal-
pi-
tate
My back arches so hard I snap in half

on the Link light rail on the way to drop
off my stuff at Rich's in Cap Hill
b4 checking in w/ Colleen b4 my reading at Mount Analogue
at ZZZ Space and IMAGINE BEING
THE MOZZARELLA IN BTWN THAT FUCKING SLICE
OF BAGUETTE R U KIDDING ME 6'8 and 6'9
I NEED TO BE IN A SMALL CLOSET IN A SHOE
BOX APT IN THE CUT OF THE STICKS
LIKE TOTALLY ALONE SUFFOCATING
INTO A PAPER BAG and Jess texts
me she's got a mass inside her the size
of an orange she's going under next
week and I'm practicing
lines

for when I officiate Becky's wedding some kind
of grand
metaphor abt the golden
hour A dappled kind of time when the sky is stained with more color
than it has at any other time of day such that light bursts through
everything Everything glows Everything haloed with light Everything
looks like a memory A kind of waltz with impermanence and supper
bells and time When even dust and clouds, those dull greys, reflect the
magic of the father of the sky When the angle of the sun to the horizon
means the light has to pass through more of Earth's atmosphere and

that compact of atmosphere filters out the blue hue light normally
emitted by the sun, giving the hour its soft and golden name That
light, that sliver of golden light, is light unlike any other light you'll
ever encounter—and that completely saturated natural light can't be
replicated by anything else Nothing we've ever made can come close to
that glow Not a filter not a software not a bulb When you rise who you
have been raised by, all the people who have angled and passed through
your life and loved you and gave you shine to make you into this person
A gathering of circumstances that produced the light of you right now in
this moment & someone tells me "You shd wait
five yrs in btwn publishing
books like what's
the
rush?"
and I'm like did u not just read? My cousin died today
and he was only two years older
than me and it's been this way my whole
life like biiiiiiiiiiiiiiiiiiiinch

I would LOVE to imagine
being alive in five
years but I have these bones u know?
and just like that I'm writing
a poem
a poem
a poem
again

The ephemerals big bloom
big beau and beautiful; sip spoonfuls of April air—the feral
perfume
Razzle dazzle and jazz cigarettes in the June
Jordan Almond afternoon

It's spring!
I'm tired of being
grave

Track 4: "Let's Talk About Sex" by Salt-N-Pepa. Except change the
lyrics to, "Let's talk about *death* baby." Underscore that you have
to sing that lyric three times in succession, to underlie that even
in the winkie-frownie up-and-down season of spring, there is some
consistency.

What a better time than in the face
of spring and the spring
ephemerals — a bloom
so
short
it puts the fleet in "fleeting feeling"
which, okay,
fleet is on sale for like 1.99 at Walgreens. Spring
cleaning, and

Track 5: "Gettin' It" by Too $hort. Mostly that part abt get it while the
gettin' is good. Cos you know why? Everyone could! You should be
too! "Pluck" is a perfectly springy word to use here. Vigor is the art he
argues for.

So much butter. Butter, butter, butter, butter, rockin everywhere am
I rite?

One stick, two stick, red stick, blue stick. I thought maybe half a stick?
No, it's half a stick for the sausages, but a whole one for the tomato
sauce. Butter the bread, get yr sea salt rocks off. The water shd taste
Atlantic. Monica's kid practically revs himself into the tabletop behind
us in her Albany Park apartment with Popeyes "come hither" musk

wafting in through the open window. Says she didn't know how to cook before she got married, that trying new dishes was a way she and her husband bonded. Keeping kids alive is some shit, I think while remembering when we'd duct tape 40s to our palms in college.

The garlic the green
pepper the onion—which! I just learned how to cut: Claw hands.
Cracked my first egg ever for a cooking show in Berkeley where I made a spaghetti and chard frittata to serve a boy the morning after we've presumably played dick-butt. The basics are my revelation. The andouille sausage, the bacon
tips, the ham hock, the scallions, the smoked
paprika bubble bubble's the gumbo in Roy's Concordia apartment by the bakery where the dad, just after a run, bought me a coffee while I was in line and slipped me his number.

The heat. The bubble bubble *infuses* Get ready
for a dead horse:

Infuse: cause to penetrate. To introduce as if by pouring. Instill. To imbue or inspire. To steep or soak (leaves, bark, root, etc.) in liquid so as to extract the soluble properties or ingredients. Late Middle English past participle of *infundere*, to pour into. In: verb formative prefix. Used to indicate inclusion. Fuse: tube, cord, or the like filled or saturated with combustible matter, for igniting an explosive. To melt under heat caused by excess current, thereby opening the circuit. To combine or blend by melting together. To become united or blended. From the Latin *fūsus*—melted, poured, cast. As in the walls are high

and hard to climb until the temp turns up
and we're flush with each other As far as I'm concerned
when it gets this hot, pant legs and sleeves are a hate
crime

I'm almost always talking *to someone but almost never* seeing *anyone,*
I say as me n Leo pass through the Chelsea Market Passage and our
voices bounce around the thrum of the crowd shuffling about us now.
Our passage between and through the gently stalling masses like an
obstacle course of bodies. *I mean the last time I really dated someone
was . . .* I look up at him while trailing off, which is becoming a pebble
feature of our patter. *Anyway, the wedding looked gorgeous, from what
I saw on Insta,* I say like a Hawaiian shirt in the winter: not quite
believable but go off. He shakes his head and eyes into me like shards
of glass. *That's not what you really think.* Stalled behind a double-wide
stroller I stop and turn to him. *Leo, for the love of god you had flip-flops
made for the guests with both yr freaking initials on them. I was praying
that I would choke to death on my own vomit so I would never have to see
it again.* Leo grins wide as the High Line. *How long are you in town for?*

If it was going to happen
it
would have happened by now right? So many ways
extraterrestrial love I mean life DOESN'T exist The unstable
axial tilt
of Mars probs why the atmosphere decayed What if, looking
into the bastion of other worlds Kepler and TESS and SETI and
METI
tinkering roving for new
Earths to exploit
Kepler 438b its orbit hospitable for liquid
water, comfortable range of temperatures OH BUT WAIT —
its host star is faaaaar too temperamental, sends out regular flares
of overwhelming radiation. Life unlikely. Next planet. Organic
compounds passing like ships in cold, dark methane skies
What if *this* is the only outpost of life? Eukaryote precarity. So what was
I saying
again? Oh yes — everything is always hungry
for something — pork, mulch, money, money, money, biiiinch

Dear reader,

can you hear the moaning
plane overhead?
Feel the beating heat
on yr t-
zone? The sizzle of foam
on the water?

Poems light up corridors of the mind, like food.

I grew up on a food
desert, a speck
of dust on the map of the United
States—an Indian reservation east of San Diego in a valley surrounded
by mountains that slice thru the clouds like a loaf
where the average age of death is 40.7 years old.

I am 34.

I live in the busiest city in America.

I am about to eat an orange.

Every feed owes itself to death. Poetry is feed
to the horses within me.

[in three voices, like a braid: Gansevoort Woodland 2]
shadbushes, Amelanchier; am-meh-LANG-kee-er
Japanese clethra, Clethra barbinervis; KLETH-ruh bar-bin-ER-vis
Dawn viburnum, Viburnum × bodnantense; vi-BER-num bod-nant-
EN-see

The ancient Egyptians used to worship cats.

And now they're dead.

[in three voices, like a braid: Washington Grassland]
Autumn moor grass, Sesleria autumnalis; sess-LAIR-ee-ah ot-um-NAL-iss
purple moor grass, Molinia caerulea; moh-LIN-ee-ah ser-OO-lee-ah
Grace smokebush, Cotinus coggygria; koe-TYE-nus kog-GIG-ree-uh
North American native smokebush, Cotinus obovatus; koe-TYE-nus
ob-oh-VAY-tus

Me n Wilkes skank down Essex on our way to the sushi place that
has the happy hour where you can get a roll for two dollars and they
always play mid-90s R&B and oftentimes in the middle of the meal
we gotta stop everything we're doing and just listen to the song not
looking at each other or anyone.
Me: Not to be a Doubting Thomas but I don't think there's a Paradox
at all. There's no *evidence* of alien civilizations because there *aren't*
any others. Maybe life is just extremely rare.
Wilkes: If it's an infinite universe, how likely is it that this is the only
planet that can sustain life?
Me: So it's just probability that keeps you believing.
Wilkes: Let's just say that the nature of intelligent civilization, one
that's been around a lot longer than us, one that's smart enough to be
aware of us, let's give them some credit. If we're not detecting them it's
because they don't want to be detected.
Me: Sure but no matter where you go, elements are all the same. Gold
and helium and shit. Space is infinite but resources aren't. In a world this
rich in resources, they would be farming the fuck out of us right now.
Wilkes: The way we're doing things, we can't last much longer as it is.
Everyone kind of knows that. Every morning I take a shower I wonder
what it's going to be like when bathing is a luxury, the way it is for so
many other people in the world. If they are older than us, they would

have had to figure out some other way of being. They would have to
be better than us, or perish.
Me: It sounds like you're saying civilization isn't inherently imperial.
Wilkes: Maybe
Me: Are you . . . an optimist?
Wilkes: So we're just throwing around the "O" word now, willy-nilly?
Enough with your sailor talk!

Dear Leo,

I mean Reader,
I will always remember You
I mean Leo
on the drive
to Seattle, platelets
in the artery of the 5 shunting

SACRAMENTO PROTESTS CONTINUE AMID POLICE
SHOOTING DEATH

into the city's heart
bc usually I take the bust
I mean bus from Portland
bc of course I'm usually by myself
and the bust
meanders off the freeway and comes
in on the sneak
dropping me in the international district
like a side piece

You showed me a new edifice of the city, a new perspective that taught
me to remember to breathe with every humor of my body. Honestly,
who tf keeps inviting pesto basil to this party, I say into my tomato

mozz breakfast sandwich that I only bought because I needed to eat
something before drinking my green tea so I wouldn't vom in the
airplane bathroom aGAIN. Which crook cook said it was okay to
put balsamic roasted red peppers and sun dried tomatoes in EVERY.
GOD. DAMNED. SANDWICH.

This is the last soupy sentiment abt boys I'll ever lip-smack into a tin
cup tethered to yr teenage bedroom
You have an impulse
says Dr. John. *It's not about forcing yrself to turn the impulse off. You
can indulge, you can not indulge. Just be curious. Look at it. You've
been a journalist. Ask it who where what why and how* Motherfucker

Plants have the most complicated biochemistry in nature—it's not
explicit, their influence, but powerful as passive aggression. Family
like a forest, like home it grows
wherever I go. Trees of forests of families gabbing at the root. Wild
tobacco developing nicotine as a toxin to shoo away insects who feed
on the leaves.

I'm hungry.
There, I said it.
I'm not taking it
back

I guess time really has passed
even tho now it feels like gurgling reedy rainbow
sprinkles I remember being a common teen
age anorexic in the throws I mean
throes of whittling myself invincible I mean
invisible and saying "I'm Hungry"
was like saying "Kill Me Slowly With Blunt
Force Trauma You Fucking Dog
Bitch"

and while I've smoothed closer
and closer
to saying *that* word and in fact all
words and in fact it turns out
I have a really loud
ass
face
underneath the mirepoix I mean three sisters
of self-censorship and x-treme self
doubt and chopped onions
Is it revolutionary, asserting the desire to continue? Well,
it certainly is new

Consume to continue
Decisive knife
Legal Weed
Saturated natural light
Morning porny wood

Is hunger something
I shd take care of with food?

Okay.
Yes.
Got it. Dear reader, let's make a culture!

Let's make a dough. Like anyone whose culture has been scrubbed
from history, you can scrub my apple crumble

But you can never scrub my hunger

Making culture is me exposing my will to live. Shhh, don't tell anyone.
Ppl think I'm a nihilist but I haven't thought abt burning it all down

for like 20 minutes now. I mean really, how can you be anything but a nihilist when you've accidentally clicked on a link to a anal prolapse vid *Really? As a person seated in shame yr about to shame?*

Let's get bubbling
Let's get wet
Let's bold the buttock loaves @ Kristina's Bernal Heights abode

Yes! I have become the kind of person who says "buttocks" instead of booty cheeks or ass clappers or pound cakes It's a new dawn it's a new day

The culture teems. I guess we shd discuss the matter of our trade-off. Ask me a question, any question that spreads the oil along yr non-stick head

No, not that one.

Not that one either.

Jesus, yr really bad at this.

What the hell is wrong with you?

Oh no, that one is beautiful, thank you love :-)

Yes I suppose I still feel in my ankle and wrist chakras
the small sand weights I wd wear to weigh-ins at the NDN clinic to make sure I didn't sliver slip lower on the scale and so my mom wd feel some stability
during the tail end of their marriage
when the sun set on our family

She sends me lists of memories
from the vagaries of her wind
Flowering moments
Mom is old, she says over text every other
day

I want someone to keep these memories after me

1985, Tekakwitha Conference in Syracuse, New York. Mohawk nation
in Kahnawake, Quebec.

Colors are innervated
daubed by millennia of associations and projective identifications
Grey is soft, limitless gush Canopy-eye
nose picker underwear riding up

1967

The year before the Olympics I remember
dropping
down
from Toluca into Mexico City
at
night
on the back of a milk
truck, glittering bowl of gems that was the skyline
The city gushed around us in constant
motion
Brash drivers thrashed the narrow streets, wound the roundabouts,
arteries
with platelets of people
from all over the world
The stately

buildings and Chapultepec Park
The hamburguesa restaurant for American touristas

We laugh.

With all the wonderful food in Mexico City,
why?

I guess everyone likes a taste of home A tint
of Adrienne Rich's
Dream of a Common Language

[in three voices, like a braid: Hudson River Overlook]
Sumacs, Rhus typhina, roos ti-FEE-na
Rhus glabra; roos GLAY-bra
mountain mint, Pycnanthemum muticum; pic-NAN-the-mum mew-
tee-CUM
Joe-Pye-weed, Eupatorium; yew-pah-TOR-ee-um
blazing star, Liatris; LYE-ah-tris

Rich and Willie and Chase twalk
about the Proud Boys
stalking up Cap Hill 70 strong twice
the size
they were last year
and I can only think how much smaller the year before that or maybe
not smaller but so much less brazen before the terracotta slob slithered
their truth

"Not to fight" Chase says intones
they're mostly non-violent frat
boys just trying to

disrupt

the

community

and I feel like a back/slash runneth thru me Blood leaking from
uncooked meat
Not like Palestine-protest-Jerusalem-embassy massacre
or in Pakistan where the journalists "disappeared"
or Mogadishu bustling city-center bombs or ICE

losing thousands of migrant kids at every
turn targeting target
rash explosion of ticks nearing Lyme season again targeting churches
Sanctuaries and Sanctuary Cities
and the bombs
and the bombs
and the bombs
fly over state drones fly over other countries

and the lol "president"
says "we" "tamed" "the" "continent"
and "we" "aren't" "apologizing"
"for" "America"
and murdered and missing indigenous women
never
ever
ever
ever
ever
ever
ever

ever
ever
ever
ever
ever
ever
ever
ever
ever
ever
ever
ever
ever
ever
ever
ever
ever
ever
ever
ever
ever
ever
ever
get an article a shout-out or a headline
but that white crisis actor lady who advocates for police brutality got
water splashed
in her face at a brunch spot Or the mouthpiece to the regime getting
denied service at a Red Hen or staffers "bummed out" at their
treatment in public
—to outcry—
and it's like idk
if I'm ever here wtf

Reconcile:
to cause
a person
to accept or to be resigned to something not desired

Mom does not want to be hooked up to no machines she texts
day after Auntie passes *That's not prolonging life that's extending death*

To win over
to friendliness; cause to be amicable.

We're on the benches. I suggested tea. I blow on mine as the swoopy
bangs blow about his face in the golden light. *I have a real
bed now, not that stupid box spring* Off-brand foam mattress
I bought in installments from Overstock with a gel
topper to whisk away the heat I trail
off into my matcha green before slicking my eyes back up to Leo's *Sorry
didn't mean for that to sound like an invitation. God, the first thing out
of my mouth is about my bed. I'm not asking you to get in it, I mean
sorry but I think we've both moved on lol I didn't want to, it's just . . .*

        *. . . after that last fight, I kept thinking about what
you said, about how I just had a box spring on the floor. I felt ashamed
like so immature you know? I've been trying ever since to grow up.
Sometimes it feels like I am. But sometimes it feels like it's everyone else
around me growing up, and I'm just getting older.*

To compose or set-
tle

I will not

DEATH TOLL IN PUERTO RICO CLOSER TO 5,000 THAN
THE OFFICIAL ACCOUNT OF 64

write about sit-ups or Pepto-Bismol

To bring into agreement or harmony, make compatible or consistent.
Reconciling the derelict railway's past to the park's future. The city to
nature. The deathless cycle of seasons to this final second. I farted
on a plane
and no matter how many air
nozzles
you open it's (the fart) not
going anywhere

From the Middle English
from the Latin

meaning to make good again. Repair. Which alludes to a previous
rupture. Breakage. We assumed that somehow just being together,
itself, was the act of repair. At one point there was a point, a

unity

a whole, something unbroken, something uniform, something together,
something that held on June 1491 Our fingers braided Skipping to the
deli in the summer song Something that leaped along the seats to greet
each other in the spring afternoons when my allergies thunderstorm'd
into full on bronchitis but I was so determined to see Beyoncé's
Lemonade in HBO realtime SIDEBAR it was cute af we made yellow
rice and plantains and vodka lemonades to keep it yellow themed.

Track 6: "Love Drought" by Beyoncé. The part that underlies a break
in the cycle, the circuit, through which all this unnoticed love leaks

out—floating in the hair I mean air. How to repair? When to care? I'm try/ing. So are you. That is the most important thing. That sometimes yr preternaturally attracted to someone, to the perfect denim jacket of their personality quirk but maybe the protein sequence never meant romantic. How could we have seen

That doesn't mean perfect. It means work.

I knew from the beginning I wasn't bringing Proxima Centauri b home mostly bc I'm sporting the largest chest zit (or chacne) in American history it's painful and cystic and volcanic and disgusting like a pepperoni pimple in between my two nipples I look like the three-tit alien from *Total Recall* but he's totally tall and striking with this long dark hair you just want to yank while he's cracker jack hammering into you while making in his mind sincere eye contact and maybe even on the edge of blurting *does it hurt? are you okay?* which, don't get ahead of yrself bud and it's got you wondering does he actually have a small penis or is this an average sized dick on a jolly green giant but somewhere in the bar crawl in your new neighborhood bc you've had to move for the like 69th time in this metropolis for the rich stupid puke town that bucks stability like, well, a buck somewhere after the second Bells Two Hearted you realize two things 1) I'm not saying Proxima Centauri b is dumb I'm not saying you can hear the ocean He just doesn't have much to say it's like he makes an echo of himself so when I say "this bar is cute" he nods and says "this bar *is* cute" or when I say that summer I lived in Columbia once there was a rainstorm so severe "a whole hillside of people died in my sleep" and he says "a whole hillside of people died wow" and 2) Stellar wind hits Proxima Centauri b at about 2k times the pressure experienced by Earth so that plus the radiation coming off its red dwarf host star has completely blown its atmosphere away making the place completely uninhabitable. Next planet.

[in three voices, like a braid: Sundeck & Water Feature]
swamp milkweed, Asclepias incarnata; uh-SKLEE-pee-us in-kar-NAY-tuh
cardinal flower, Lobelia cardinalis; lo-BEE-lee-ah kar-din-AL-iss
bitter panicgrass, Panicum amarum; PAN-ih-kum ah-MAR-um
white turtlehead, Chelone glabra; keh-LOE-nee GLAY-bruh

I'm nervous

where I feel

most

free

A fuss

in my noggin
like a bell with a big dong until I can't hear anything else. The wave
pulls back on the sand, the sand suddenly alive with crawlers *It's like
you were raised around zombies or something* Leo said, spread out on the
towel and slathering sunscreen on my neck my back. *You got out, right?
You survived the zombie apocalypse but yr afraid you got bit or something,
that the virus or whatever, their virus, circulates in you.* In the distance, a
kid watches his sandcastle battered by the waves. He delights.

My spirits are protective
of me They're above me now, a cloud of light plugged
into my back I wanted to stay alive and now they feed me and flow out
of my hands This
was our vow — but sometimes the vows you take to stay
protected came at a time when you were particularly

78 MILLION ACRES OF OUR OCEANS OPENED UP FOR OFFSHORE DRILLING

vulnerable. Necessarily. My spirits surround me like a cloud of
disapproving aunties, keeping most of you at bay. A childhood merged
into my love-space So compacted, that compartment Is there room
for a lover I mean agar-agar from the algae
make a powder
make me thickly Dear reader,

Are letters a repository for all the things I'm *going* to say to you, or the
things I can *never* say to you? Prepare

the ingredients separately before throwing them together. Follow
the course of the recipe like a mnemonic device Hand me
the thermometer and bend over Oh, you didn't know?
We're getting hitched! You mud-puddling this far is basically
a marriage contract. We're seeing each other thru. It's the only
shade of commitment I can offer you.

Once I dated a dude who made scents for fun.

Unlike taste, which is largely innate, he said rising up from the foam
bed in his Hollister skivvies in the Taaffe Lofts off Classon, *smell is
more associative.* When he made scents he talked in metaphors and
it made me love him more. *This one,* he said tincture dropping onto
a blotter then offering it up to me like a prayer, *I call* The Sky Is Blue
and Mom Is Sad

His low barrel baritone vibrating
in harmony with the din of A/C him crackling
through me. I brewed him
a jalapeño infused whiskey

a week before his birthday
but he dumped me
on text the next day

I drank the whiskey.

Next planet.

I say, "it's fine." I say
"some things need to be boiled
in order to release
their flavor."

Bonito flakes.
The meat relaxes.
The meat the blood The leeks are almost done!

Preheat the oven to 420 degrees.
Wash the bird and remove its innards and cut
off
all the schmaltz.

Oil literally everything.
Stuff garlic, onion, and quartered lemon into the cavity

Spread the rigid cubes of sweet potatoes and bunched
brussels sprouts
around the pan
Pepper and salt liberally
Sprinkle with thyme

Avoid making stupid thyme puns like thyme after thyme, or thyme is
on my side, or right in the nick of thyme, or thyme waits for no one, or

thyme's up! or thyme out New York, or if I could turn back thyme, or I've had the thyme of my life and I never felt this way before, or thyme warp, or thyme in a bottle, or I got that summerthyme summerthyme sadness, thyme and thyme again, first thyme I ever saw yr face, thymes they are a changin, it's the most wonderful thyme of the year, it's the thyme of the season when love runs high, love me two thymes, or once, twice, three thymes a lady—be a gd adult.

Jess pulls meat from the ribcage
like her grandmother
The most flavorful parts are

closest

to the bone. Everything smells
like fuzzy comfort

A season used to be an authority figure

WHALE DIES IN THAILAND AFTER SWALLOWING 80
PLASTIC BAGS

but now I can get tomatoes anytime of the year

Alaska Air. MetroLink. MTS. BC Ferries.

Don't fuck
with those boys
in San Francisco, they're all vers tops
until the red light
comes
on

Girl

careful with those boys
in LA, make plans
all night
and forget how to text
all day

Can I just say!
Seattle is a trick
cos all the boys wanna wear nail

polish but none of them want to suck dick

Candlelight is not too poetic to mention in a poem if we say the light
slicks across our faces like mud butt.

The candlelight slicked across our faces like mud butt. If I'd have
known that was the last time I'd see his face lit at night I might
have paid attention to the tall shadows. Cast, like a line. Catching
connection. The ancestors say, *sit up straight.*

He "did" sales. Spent our dates polishing the poop chute of his
attributes. *I'm a people person* he said over soggy vinegar and mayo
fish n chips. *Sales is about being a good listener,* he'd coo into my ear
after he picked my napkin off the floor and glossed it across my lap. *I
think . . . I think my worst quality is that I'm too real, I speak my mind
too much,* he said unprompted. He was like 6'5. His arms

made me want to throw myself
down
a flight of stairs. Touch crazed, I'd burrow
into bed, my mind alive with whatever the word

is when you can't olive oil NO—when you and sleep
are like oil and water. I'd burrow
into bed, calmed by even the idea of him around
me, calmed so completely that all my sighs
came out in shudders and pies. But the days
and weeks wore without momentum. We drive to the light-
house Mimosa flute bodies clink cheers salud Then he drove
me home. Drop off the same time every night Arms
stay an idea. His arms abstract. So I

go
Lighting the horizon line like always. I go
and it's far.

Day 69 of tour:

TTC. STM. A Streetcar Named I'm Tired.

YES
I'm going to Diet Coke break eat
a hot dog to the gods
in front of these cat-
calling construction workers while making smoky eye
contact until they look

away

Yeah yeah yeah yeah yeah yeah
I'm gonna eat a banana at Star
bucks square
stance
in front

of the man who painstakingly ordered
his half caff two pump vanilla chai double
sweet extra hot espresso shot latte HOLY
FUCK JAMES COMEY IS 6'8 TSA regulations

state

you can have one
carry-on bag and one
personal item only.
All other bags need to be checked

oh and drop
dead.

Hey,
morning.
Do you want to get breakfast or something?
At least a coffee? What is the difference

between being alone
and being

lonely?

Track 7: "Hold On, We're Going Home" by Drake. Ignore the music
video entirely. I mean really, it's paternalistic garbage take my word for
it or don't. Focus on the super earnest part that feels real af rn about
how hard it is to do "these things" alone. Less survivor's guilt and more
I'm thriving guilt
Alone

is the physical
feeling, literal proximity

just not being around other bodies

Lonely

is a desire, the urge
for a companion or sympathetic
compatibility.

Something on the other side of the country.
Something shivering or
like
feeling incomplete

right?

(But there are so many people inside me.)

Is this a recapitulation of that Aristophanes myth?

It doesn't feel worth it to spit
the ins and outs of the conflict
As if there could be
any other
way.

FINE, twist my arm you bullies I'll put on pants. What happened
was the train was killing
people. It wasn't exactly a speed demon
AND there was a man on horseback waving red
ahead

of the train and still it was killing people all along tenth
avenue, or death
avenue as it was known

So they lifted it—up the ladder to the roof—raised the train line High
Line, a hanging monument to the appetite of the sky

Track 8: "Heartbeats" by The Knife (or honestly the José González
cover but I'm a sucker for Karin Dreijer). Am I the only one who
thinks this song is about atheism? Focus on the part where she sings
that calling on hands from above for stability, to "lean on," isn't good
enough for her. Hands of above? No, I need the hands right in front.
Maybe the hands under. Hands around. But not hands of above.
Prayer never helped nobody do nothing.

30 feet in the rowdy
air, overlooking the yearly city sea change of

Lenape

land

and the river, the farmers markets into printing presses into art
galleries, it was called "the life line of New York" because it was built
in part to transport milk, butter, eggs, meat, and cheese from farms
upstate into the city.

On the ground, the last man on horseback to precede the train down
the avenue waved through fourteen freight cars filled with oranges.
After decades of life, in 1980 the final

chug

on the High Line train were three boxcars filled with turkeys for
Thanksgiving Day.

After almost 30 years
of being

abandoned

the wild line I mean High Line became an accidental meadow
of roses
ailanthus trees
dandelions
Virginia creeper
black cherry
chives
Queen Anne's lace A wild, edenic recapturing of neglect
The park itself is a version of this, a matrix design
of microclimates in layered
associations that approximate the wilderness
with wildness, a curated dance of plant surprises — the shadbush
vibrating its hue from apricot to dogwood. The gardens stay
unfinished. The buildings grow and grow their spears of shade over the
park where some grasses persist, others thrive, and some just die.

[in three voices, like a braid: Northern Spur]
skyblue aster, Aster azureus; ASS-tur a-ZUR-ee-us
Pennsylvania sedge, Carex pensylvanica; KAIR-ecks pen-sill-VAY-nih-
kuh
wild-oat, Chasmanthium latifolium; kaz-MAN-thi-um lat-ih-FOE-lee-
um
Indian physic, Porteranthus stipulatus; pour-ter-AHN-thus try-foe-lee-
AY-tuh

Ok so in Plato's *Symposium*
the philosopher Aristophanes makes
this speech at some white
robe
sweaty ball
table linen dinner
about the origin of love.

That at one point
there were three sexes:
the children of the sun (two men)
the children of the earth (two women)
and the children of the moon (man and woman)
attached at the back

Now before you get all
sapiosexual
on me, I don't know this from Plato

I know this from *Hedwig and the Angry Inch*

N E WAYS, so yeah at one point
the three sexes were whole
round balls
adherent to each
other attached at the back and spinning

in their own orbit.

The problem
was people

GUNMAN FIRES INTO OKLAHOMA CITY RESTAURANT

were too
content in self-possession

there was no ambition no thrill of the chase
no colonialism. So the gods split
the people down the back
and ever since we've been looking
for our other
half

Lonely as a kind of math.

Track 9: "Electric Feel" by MGMT. Sub in the Justice remix if yr
feeling festive (you can thank me later). First things first, change the
pronoun from "girl" to "boy." Ooh, boy. That's that ecstatic touch, I
need some grounding. Tried to get into new MGMT but the first song
is called "She Works Out Too Much" and I was like, nah I'm good.

Me n Wilkes wait outside the burrito restaurant for the rest of our
party to arrive and it is in fact the place with the burritos so hefty
Nalini calls them "food tubes" so usually I just get the flautas and 52
strawberry margaritas but we're not even annoyed to be waiting outside
because it's still the part in spring where a night warm enough to be
outside without a space suit is a revelation and a blessing, and because
even though neither of us is sentimental enough to say anything: she is
glad I'm back home and I'm glad to be back, too.
Me: They say Ross 128 b is one of the most Earth-like exoplanets
we've come across, but it revolves around a red dwarf star which—75%
of stars in the sky are red dwarf stars. And because they're so much
smaller and cooler than the sun, a planet in the habitable zone gotta
be very close to it. Way more close than the Earth
Wilkes: What are you getting at
She leans back on the round NYC bike rack, careful to hover a half

inch in her white sheath dress with the red buckle and black polka dots.
Me: If you're that close to your parent star, the gravity involved means
you're tidally locked with one half of the planet permanently—
Wilkes: Yr not gonna catch me off guard this time, Teebs. I did my
research and the Internet said: Do you know this thing called the Drake
equation?
I shake my head no in a way that suggests, "math? really?!" in my
oversized blue striped sweater and short-shorts which is my fall specialty
I call it the *Empire Records* Liv Tyler look
Wilkes: There are between 100 and 400 billion stars in our galaxy.
Billion! And for each one of these stars in our galaxy, there IS a galaxy
in our observable universe. The moooost conservative scientific
estimate is that 5% of those stars are sun-like, and the most conservative
estimate is that of those sun-ish stars, 22% of those might have Earth-
like worlds. That means 100 billion-billion Earth-like worlds exist out
there. You mean to tell me, you have the complete hubris to believe we
are the only outpost of LIFE?
Me: The whole observable universe though? The chances of us making
contact with another solar system in our galaxy versus one seven
galaxies over? That's all within yr Googles huh?
Wilkes: Let's just say in our galaxy, if 1% of Earth-like planets develop
life and 1% of *those* develop a kind of "civilization," in our galaxy of
100 billion stars, that means 1 billion Earth-like planets and 100,000
intelligent civilizations exist in our own galaxy. My good bitch.
Me: Then I'm gonna echo our dude Fermi on this one: Where *is*
everybody?

The idea
is that a "true self" exists somewhere below the layers and layers of scarves—
all squishy eternity and Cèdre Atlas Atelier toilet water

and in the contour, a false self
The persona

we create to conform to society
Maison de Parfum

On persona, George Orwell says, "The job is to reconcile my
ingrained likes and dislikes with the essentially public, non-individual
activities that this age forces on all of us. It is not easy. It raises
problems of construction and of language, and it raises in a new way
the problem of truthfulness." What would George Orwell say about
Twitter. If you're going to ask that, what would Susan Sontag write
about Instagram.

I've got Swedish Fish in my bag.

Swag.

"Kellyanne Conway is the biggest leaker in the White House" blares
across the MSNBC ticker tape and gd it that intern deserves a job.

A hot person farts on the tarmac and gets super embarrassed and I'm
like *this is what it sounds like when doves cry*

Fear me, beer me, from the rear me.
Island of the Bi Dolphins.
Attila the Pun.

Dear reader,

the truth is: I don't understand
I'm onstage every other night Sprite
from college classroom to community center auditorium to main
street bookstore to makeshift poetry library in an artist's loft to bar
backyard after hrs Chinese resto weird laundromat vivid variety show
at the venue where R.E.M. got its start

Around more people than I've ever been
in my whole life but I've never been
so

CTA. MTA. the Metro. the Metro-North. Link light rail.

lonely.

Joe says it's a quintessential
American narrative—success that doesn't lance
to happiness

Dear reader, don't stone me for this:

My apartment is centrifugal force, the tug
of turning a corner on a
narrow
road I fall asleep in the hum of a grey
thin sleeveless hoodie Wake
up in Philly, fully Teebs

The road performs
a smile stretched over the drum of my
"prepare a face to meet the faces you will meet"
Teebs-inflated, it's like the other "me" watches from the sunken
place pushes
that "true self"
deeper dapper down deep
until it's like I gotta Dwayne the Rock Johnson
myself out of a crevasse in the

Himalayas

via super dramatic helicopter rescue

Do you think Selena
hears our

prayers?

Is she somewhere eating a whole medium pizza by herself?
In that way, doing something

alone

is an accomplishment
A self-reliance
Hands to the sky
Assurance of the appetite
My father is drunk flailing incoherent pissed but weak on Old English
and my mother has him pinned against the wall so we could leave to
Auntie's place but We keep coming back We keep coming back We
Keep We Keep We and looking up at her I knew the story recycles
because it's love that makes you weak

Does it all have to be codependency or isolation? Dr. John says

Couldn't there be a green valley in between
these polar vortexes
hexes
exes
The echo
Another illusion that yr not alone

Track 10: "I'm Not In Love" by 10cc, which, the 10cc entries in
karaoke are . . . polarizing. So in this song: He loves you, but he'll

never tell you in fact he'll flat out deny it. It's just a silly phase he's
going through. He cares so much he'll never let you know. That
picture of you he likes? Just hiding a stain. A Nasty stain. He doth
protest let me tell
you

I'm in loathe w/ him & Dr. John asks me, *why do u ass-*
u-
me
Teebs is the false self?
Why do u ass-
u-
me
The shy thing The polite thing The hide behind a parent's leg thing
The inside voice thing The scooped shoulders thing
The *oh stop I'm worthless I'm sorry for breathing* thing
is your lol truth? What if letting out the Teebs is reconnecting to the
monkey bar swing singer before shame shame knew your name?

Do you want to start a honey
flavored THC candy
business with me called
All I Wanna Do Is Get High by the Bee Get High by the Bee Get High?

Do you want to start a line
of makeup
specifically
for the pubic region called
Beat Around the Bush?

Do you want to star
in a PBS documentary
short with me called

Hells Angels in America?
It's mostly about the mid-90s Jim Carrey movie *Liar Liar*.

Dear reader,

Once again I don't know where

the feeling is or what to do with it

and spent most of the day in bed with my eyes squeezed shut—
everything all over the news feed and the names the names The list
of the newest mass shooting on record the names the list of shooting
victims of fragile masculinity and misogyny and a rigged system in favor
of assault rifles over human life Where bathrooms are a battleground
Pundits and politicians warn that MEN IN DRESSES WILL
ASSAULT WOMEN Remarkably silent on a convicted rapist being
sentenced to only three months One of the 3% of men who actually
see jail time for sexual assault bc his father says his life shouldn't be
forfeit for "20 minutes of action" and then gets let out early on "good"
"behavior" Meanwhile every stranger who starts trending is black and
shot by the cops and PRESIDENTIAL TAX FRAUD and TRADE
WAR and Is Colonizing Mars the Most Pressing Concern of "Our"
"Time"? VICTIMS OF GANG VIOLENCE IN EL SALVADOR
HAVE THEIR CHILDREN TORN AWAY AT THE BORDER

Shake off the fuck bois—masturbate, don't equivocate

[in three voices, like a braid: 10th Avenue Square]
trifoliate maples, Acer triflorum; ASS-er tri-FLOOR-um
Purple milkweed, Asclepias purpurascens; ass-CLEE-pee-us per-per-
ASS-ens
big bluestrem, Andropogon gerardii; an-droh-POH-gon jer-AR-dee-eye

I'm back
in town
for a spell
& He asks me, what's something
you learned embarrassingly
late
in life?

That it's called "spur of the moment" not "sperm
of the moment"

(but high key shouldn't
it be sperm of the moment? Cos it's like, spurt spurt spurt.)

It's deeply
life
to hold, gem-like,
a furtive crush on a tall
hottie boom body for five years of heady

static

before you *finally* start
guap-guap talking
and gazing across a taco shop
and vigorously fiddling
diddles
only to learn in three weeks
he's skipping
the country for six months
to do like charcoal blind contour drawings or something in an airless
basement in Copenhagen

and two weeks before *he* gets
back *you're* huff huffin
to the other
side
of the country for a year or maybe forever you haven't figured it out yet
bc not figuring it out yet is kind of your *thing*

like mango margaritas, tex mex on the beach
and stigmata
and THEN and THEN and THEN

he's going off to hunt for orchids
in Madagascar for three years
and it's like

UUGGGGGHHHHHH

How does everyone know the word "tetralogy" but me
of COURSE not him nor him nor
him nor him
yr old shelves dissolving old shore shetticoats to sharadise

Track 11: "Ready for the Floor" by Hot Chip. I'll have to ask Dr. John
if this counts as a Freudian slip, but I always thought the song was
like, "open up, we're tall!" And I was like f yeah! Don't be a wallflower,
come smooch me or whatever cos we're both tall! But apparently it's
"open up with talk" which okay fine dialogue or whatever. Also I love
myself a micro changing chorus. "Ready for the Floor" as in of course
dance floor or whatever, in the context of the chorus ready to talk
ready for dialogue, but when it switches to "ready for a fall" I kind of
turn into a Pisces. I . . . fall . . . to Pisces? Sorry, Patsy Cline's zombie is
like rolling around in its grave rn I'll see myself out.

Dear reader,

Yr easy to love but hard to get close to

The tarot blares The palm reader traces a line
of stormy wrinkles, face
a tea-stained gathering cloud

of COURSE
yr gonna wind
up

alone

forever rubbing yr toes together
and eating peach gummies in a rocking
chair
existentially

I finally OKAY BULLIES I finally read *Paterson* and *The Argonauts*
and *Battlefield Where the Moon Says I Love You* and *Don't Let Me Be
Lonely* and *Hard Country* and *Vanishing-Line* and *Collected Works of
Billy the Kid* and *Coeur de Lion* and *À la recherche du temps perdu* all
these tomes forever recommended that I called dubious but I call due
diligence My Lineage
Fixated on what I've inherited and what I share

It's like this whole
thing about being
"with" somebody is a game of wack-a-mole
and it's deeply wack
and Mole
dribbles

down
my chin thing on the date
where we say *everything's*
okay it's not like we're dying

we're just in between a cock and a hard
place.

And yeah rejection, chronically, can be a tool of character building
and totes unavoidable and a temporary butcher knife strike to the
chest, but

god

damn

talk about a feeling that makes you want to rip
off your own skin and flush
it down the toilet

Maybe I really am ~~Teebs~~ Box of Wine?

Anybody got a pack of matches?
Cos I feel like burning a bridge

Track 12: "Shout" by Tears for Fears. First of all, best band name in
America. Second, how cathartic am I right? Really, just let it all out.
What else can you do in an intractable situation but shout? Focus
on that full throaty wail where Roland Orzabal reveals that he's just
waiting for the lover to open up for the destruction his love will no
doubt wreak.

Dear reader

Insulin is a polypeptide hormone produced by the beta cells of the islets of Langerhans of the pancreas, tiny islands that regulate the metabolism of sugar in the blood. Insulin resistance begins when too many sugars are introduced too often into the body—the beta cells shoot their load so often the body is like, *damn insulin! Why are you so obsessed with me?*

Undigested sugar molecules rage around the blood, doing all sorts of crimes

Insulin, from the Latin *insula*: isle

Island—sugar—

Insula: a smattering of convulsions situated at the base of the lateral fissure of the brain

Dad's hair started to fall out. His long black trickster locks Tufts of it in the trash on the brush

Auntie's sister goes in to get her foot cut off

Auntie goes in for dialysis. They told her stick a needle in the orange for practice. It's porous, like skin. *Auntie, you've been injecting the orange this whole time? What the heck?*

I am the recipe I protect.

How much can you rely on being alive tomorrow

I don't really like this full pastoral
bull
but I actually do really miss holding hands with Leo
on the way to
on the way to
on the way to the waterfront to stuff our faces with tapas which I said
were my favorite genre of food because I like to spread myself
thin
and I have commitment issues His arm around my shoulders in my
red satin Artful Dodger baseball jacket with the sun pitting into the
mountains of tenements and the galleries and the museums and the
garages and the condos and the empty prison of the Meatpacking
District visible from the walk and all these teens who weirdly just
witness our love without jeering Taking care of our city moment

Track 13: "You're Makin' Me High" by Toni Braxton. Have you ever
listened to a song casually for fifteen years and then one day at karaoke
at that laser booth in Koreatown where they give you a tambourine
and shrimp chips you read the lyrics flashing across the screen and go
oh . . . my . . . god. This is *naaasty!* lol Get lifted in the presence.

Of course all those beers later when Leo sprang fully formed from the
Chelsea Thicket w/ his pastel grin and me tickled hippo pink The
whole ribbon of time just
unraveled
and all I wanted to do was rebozo wrap him around me Wear his
dusky musk Whip kisses on his biceps and flick the dick of his nose.
Dick nose We're at a funeral

My mother's red satin-ish Wild Bunch baseball jacket Every rez in
the county had a team And it's raining It's a closed casket and I'm 4 I
fleshy count out my fingers to my relatives when they ask They make
the big eyes like they never seen a kid demanding attention before like
they still believe in the promise of our ancestors and I do it on a garish

loop bc it makes them laugh. I'm one, two, three, four! I affect their affected surprise back to them, like an echo of a banana splat. I'm like a rodeo clown but for funerals trying to distract my relatives from their landing pad in sad Somehow I understand that fleshy love led them to this place of devastation I don't exactly swear to never do *it* but *it* becomes something I clock Cutting

is decisive and precise. In what other context do you get to grip a knife like you do when preparing ceviche. Prep is so violent, right?

Scrape out the tomato
Smash the lemons and the limes
Rip off the shrimp tails
Slice open the cucumber, the onions, the chilies into smaller and smaller minces

Simple ingredients orchid the kitchen-thing: an hour among the citrus and the onions and the cucumber and the chilies, shrimps bud from sickly grey to scrumptious punky pink

Dear reader,

It's about family. Everything's about family if you have enough string. Sitting in yr little chair while aunties flutter about the stove, the butcher block, the cutting board. We're a country club in Durango. We're a wedding cake in Mexico City. We're a hole in the wall in Tijuana.

Btw why's it called a pie-hole? Why not a stew-hole? Or a hoagie-hole? Or a roe-hole? Apparently imagination is the wages of dessert culture.

Me n Becky nibble De La Rosa cookies and blast La India, art denaturing our circuit of grey matter.

[in three voices, like a braid: Chelsea Grasslands]
Indian grass, Sorghastrum nutans; sor-GAS-trum newtons
switchgrass, Panicum virgatum; panic-UM ver-GATE-um
autumn moor grass, Sesleria autumnalis; sess-LEER-ee-uh autumn-
NAY-lus

It's my third date with Wolf 1061c and I'm scrubbed head-to-butt
because while there's been backyard-bar heavy-petting and a make
out sesh, we've yet to "do the deed" as the kids say and my real estate
needs it and I have this thought while getting ready While exfoliating
and pomading and cramming my hooves into the tight brown boots
that python the shit out of my feet but turn every sidewalk into the
runway of the century: *this whole dating thing is actually great for me*
like, ritualizing "getting ready" the way I heart-eye-emoji'd my mom
at the vanity fascinated at the magic of becoming the stepping-out
version of yrself but then Wolf 1061c shows up rough, confessing
that he was still hung over, weary-eyed, flecks of dried white spittle
in the corners of his mouth *It was really hard to get off the couch and
come out here* he says while we wait for the popcorn I have another
thought: *this whole dating thing is going to run my self-confidence out
of town on a rail* and to make matters worse he keeps talking about
his perfect ex and his perfect ex's perfect beard kind of looking into
the buzzing subway light, far far away You see it turns out while Wolf
1061c is technically in the habitable zone around its star, it lies in the
inner edge and is therefore tidally locked, one side permanently facing
the star and one side permanently dark, which means the only place
liquid water might exist is along the thin terminator line that is the
suture of the dark side and the light and you know what? I'm just not
about that stryfe. Next planet.

What if we are the only outpost of life?

Just June Jordan yr way
through small bright affairs
Buck the notion of ugh
"true love."

But what if I do wanna find the heat with somebody?

It's CORNY

When yr jib job is to zigzag around the glib globe
it's impossible
to build a temple
with anyone. All you get
are the brief blips in Texas
I mean taxes
I mean texts, bending
like plants toward the neon bar Starlight

MASS GRAVES OF IMMIGRANTS FOUND IN TEXAS

for taco Tuesdays. Maybe the argument is her audience closes
the circuit Vigors the loop An inflation that normal life siphons away

Track 14: "XO" by Beyoncé. When everything else goes dark, she
looks into the faces of the crowd—it's all she can see. Focus on the
micro change in the chorus: *You* give *me* everything. The dark is, in
fact, teeming with life. The reciprocity.

I can't help but get the beeline
I mean feeling that Beyoncé tamps herself
down
around Jay to not overwhelm the world
with her ocean I opened

my mouth and dust plumed out
years before the petrichor
I smelled it miles away I just knew
it I just knew I would also

PRO-GUN RUSSIAN BOTS FLOOD TWITTER AFTER MASS
SHOOTING

flood

Bags from the bodega in the canopy of cum
trees A webbing
from heaven
in another town I don't set
down
I don't call
home.

Susan Cain says, "In our culture, snails are not considered valiant
animals—we are constantly exhorting people to 'come out of their
shells'—but there's a lot to be said for taking your home with you
wherever you go."

Track 15: "Papa Was A Rollin' Stone" by the Temptations. When yr
stories about a person come secondhand. Companion song to "Missing"
by Everything But The Girl, both focused on the one who left. I mean
I guess papa was resilient in the sense that home was wherever he went,
just without his family. The kid's inheritance after papa died? Alone.

Oh, the markets in Mexico are amazing Blue is fluid
and compassionate
The sky so blue with clouds close and puffy like a child's drawing

Here in Guadalajara the market is three stories. We buy smoked
salmon, limes, and tortillas for a few pesos and it feeds
us on the road for several days
The market
in Acapulco. Here we find strawberry cake
tamales and deep-fried rice
tacos sprinkled with sugar. We sleep
on the beach one night and wake up to find the sand
covered with rat
prints
We're told they live in the palm
trees and come out at night
to scavenge crumbs on the beach. Food stands
everywhere. My first street
taco was in Santa Ana, in the Sonoran
Desert

Flour tortilla and beef
Cut up fruit, mostly mangoes and papayas,
watermelon or pineapple, sprinkled with chili
powder and fresh lime

Mmm, pineapple. My favorite breakfast.

Tamales, tortas, empanadas, fresh helados Vendors line
the bus and train stations selling through windows Oaxaca,
food
food
food
Papas fritas tacos Scrambled eggs in chili
sauce with beans and cheese Tamales wrapped in banana
leaves, close to the coast the blue gleaming
coast Frothy hot chocolate Dark

mole Crispy roasted grasshoppers in the zócalo in Oaxaca
City. Michoacán the creamy emerald The pyramid
at Pátzcuaro lake Morelia, colonial city, this wonderful
family—you see we
were so tired and broke
and hungry
They gave us money for the bus, sent us
on our way with love. A woman on the crowded
bus, sleeping child wrapped
in her brilliant rebozo
On the road to Acapulco we catch
a ride with a truck
driver. We stop at a ramada by the side
of the road to eat
The ladies try to teach me to make corn
tortillas. We laugh so much, the dough, sticking to my hands
never makes it to the comal. Tepic and Nayarit
and the river,
bathing finally.
Laughing as the crowd gathers on the bridge to watch
Loco Americanos
Fresh zest
after our long walk and the long ride hitchhiking We gather
our things from the riverbank and move on,
waving at the crowd. Buenos suerte! They yell
and wave back. Laughing. Waves lapping Crash A crush
of bedrock
to resist the crush of time

I'm trying over these last years to fiddle-faddle
my thoughts into the salad spinner for you son

[in three voices, like a braid: Chelsea Thicket]
American holly, Ilex opaca; EYE-lex oh-PA-cah
Emerald Sentinel red cedar, Juniperus virginiana; joo-NIP-er-us ver-
jin-ee-AY-nuh
winter hazel, Corylopsis spicata; kor-i-LOP-sis spi-KAH-ta

What's this town called?
I'm not asking you
I'm asking them:

The Ohlone. Costanoan, Muwekma. Duwamish, Suquamish,
Muckleshoot. Shawnee. Lenni-Lenape. Tocobaga, Mocoso, Pohoy,
Uzita. Lumbee, Piscataway, Nacotchtank. Multnomah. Anishinaabe.
Ojibwa, Ottawa, Potawatomi.

Dear reader,
I can't stand
in front of the audience
in Columbus, Ohio, without wondering
how that last person felt leaving
the ancestral
homeland
for the Indian
territory

and You did this to me

What is the difference between being alone and being

lonely?

Alone

is a physical
feeling, literal proximity

Just not being around other bodies

Lonely

is a desire, the urge
for a companion or sympathetic compatibility
Something on the other side
of the country. Something shivering
or like
feeling incomplete, right?

(But there are so many people inside me.)

The Earth Similarity Index (ESI) is a number calculated from an
exoplanet's radius, density, surface temperature, and escape velocity.
It ranges from 0 to 1, and any planet above a score of .8 could be
considered "Earth-like." So we find an exo-planet Luyten b. All these
classifications telling us how its orbit is hospitable for liquid water, that
it likely has a comfortable range of surface temperatures. Potentially a
rocky world, around a quiet star not regularly sending out solar flares.
Then it turns out his favorite book on OkCupid is *Atlas Shrugged*.
Can't do it sorry Next planet.

We're halfway through three thoroughly dirty martinis that he's paying
for because he's a lawyer and is like "oh you're just a writer, I've got
this" like I'm a hobby, which I suppose writing is for people who
don't do it very well but I digress I'm doing my wet eyes when he
takes a look at me like he's seeing me for the first time and confesses,
"my partner and I are looking for a third," which he'd carefully not
mentioned before and it's like ok girl next planet.

The Gaia hypothesis offers that climate change and the rise of
civilizations are intimately linked, that life has a necessary impact
on its environment. That on any planet, anywhere, at any time,
"civilization" will always cause an Anthropocene. There will always
come a reckoning. Termite ridden ships of planets sinking to the
bottom of the rocky sea of the galaxies.

Let's consult the oracle
shall we? *Webster's Dictionary* defines

a fart as an intransitive verb meaning to expel intestinal gas from the
anus, often vulgar. From the Middle English *ferten, farten*; akin to
Old High German (not unlike the dude I blew at the abandoned park
in Prenzlauer Berg) *Ferzan*, to break wind. Old Norse *freta*, Greek
perdesthai, Sanskrit *pardate*, he breaks wind. First known use: 13th
century.

I'm pardating all over
this Virgin America Metro
North Port Authority What can I say
there's something about a man 6'6 and over
that makes me want to confess my guts
out all the feelings normally lock-
and-car-keyed in the boot
of my body, like some kind of common lover
It's deeply whatever I eat
another banana w/ bullseye eyes trained on the thighs
of his face
by which I mean his eyes Nursery Web Spiders
Pisaura mirabilis
in southern Europe grow in the summer,
hibernate in winter, reach adulthood in spring,
reproduce and then die

ORLANDO POLICE TESTING AMAZON'S REAL-TIME FACIAL
RECOGNITION

in the fall During mating the male presents some nummy nums
to the female before committing thanatosis,
aka "playing possum," to avoid being eaten
during sex I was like, *wouldn't she just eat him anyway?*
But apparently most predators only want live prey

(PS: remember when Martin called Cole "Thicky Ricardo"?)

Some things you prefer to do

alone

like shit. Some things you prefer
to be appreciated
Like a fart
I mean wit Accidentally
typo'd "author" to "authot" so guess I'm an au-thot now

Track 16: "I'm So Lonesome I Could Cry" by Hank Williams. No
comment.

This is going to sound like an inelegant
complaint but I've grown road weary khaki thin
sleeveless hooded t-shirt city made of strangers
Strange woodgrain shapes in the shadowy penis
of the city night Everyone
I see these days
is someone I've known for 20 minutes
which frankly isn't enough
time

to take off the strings, to stop tap
dancing along a joke
or an anecdote

Honestly what do you expect? I'm not saying yr broken but I'm saying
you've fragmented The compartments you've created to hold the
different parts of yourself leave you fully jigsaw'd YES the standard
of the ancestors is high, but they take their cue from you Imagine a
yellow light around you This is a light of your making The ancestors
have gifted your hands with the contours of words bursting from your
finger ends *It sounds* Dr. John says, putting down his notebook to buzz
in the next appointment, *like you don't trust yourself*

Shark in the sea
an approximation
Effigy
a series of gels Chris Kraus crisscrossing Kriss
Kross'll make you jump, jump Palimpsest
style until

a version
of my color stands
in line behind you at the Boston
Market in the college town
at the bookstore
in the city
where the only other thing I've seen is the airport and the backseat
and the backhand of waiting to red eye check-in on zero sleep

See, this all sounds like an inelegant
complaint, "inelegant,"

which itself is a stubby snout
of a word. The bombs in Austin
and Flint water
keeps
comin

I had just crept into a warm robe, from the memory of a warm bath
in the warm NDN casino hotel room on an unseasonably cold day,
splayed on the still-made light lavender-grey queen, just me and the
tine of a personal cheese pie and a Vinho Verde robotically clicking
thru late night cable TV pundit comedians and reality housewives
when Wilkes facetimes me and it's so jarring I immediately reject
and text her "wtf FACEtime? are u actively trying to torpedo this
frondship?" "Ask Siri where's hell, and go there" she shoots back
a smooth 12 minutes later. "That was a tote bag dial" and even so,
I'm freaking delighted out of my gourd. I got it, the life I wanted.
Leapfrogging gig to gig not worried if I'm gonna make rent—a profesh
yarn-spinner. I just wish
my friends cd be here.

My mom is the one who got me into The Cranberries in the first place,
which makes me very cool. We converted our garage into an art studio
where she'd turn paintings and sculptures into sound installations to the
tune of "Hollywood" off *To the Faithful Departed* or "How" off *Everyone
Else Is Doing It, So Why Can't We*. It's no wonder she loved all these
songs about love and breakups and like refugees and the ozone layer but
then again the acorn doesn't fall too far from the oak tree

Cranberries, of the subgenus Oxy-CO-ccus of the genus Vax-IN-ium,
in North America probably refers to Vaccinium mac-ro-CAR-pon. The
day I read about Dolores O'Riordan's death the songs all come back
like a bullet the songs I haven't listened to since my parents split up and
my mom would lock herself in the studio blaring the songs so loud you

can't think of anything else and I'd crumple in the frame, cheek flush
against the other side of her closed door

[in three voices, like a braid: Meadow Walk]
purple moor grass, Molinia caerulea; mo-LEE-nee-uh cuh-ROO-lee-uh
Korean feather-reed grass, Calamagrostis brachytricha; cally-ma-
GROSS-tuss brack-ee-TRY-ka
bright yellow fernleaf yarrow, Achillea filipendulina; ack-uh-LEE-uh fill-
uh-pen-doo-LINE-uh

Listening to a podcast on malnutrition
at the Whole Foods
hashtag late stage capitalism

[in three voices, like a braid: Flyover]
bigleaf magnolia, Magnolia macrophylla; magnolia macro-FYE-luh
umbrella magnolia, Magnolia tripetala; magnolia try-PET-ah-luh
sweetbay magnolia, Magnolia virginiana; magnolia vur-jin-ee-AY-nuh

"Ben Affleck's Massive Back Tattoo Mocked"

lol, good one CNN. Who cares about the "president's" unconstitutional
shenanigans and the NDAs and the NRAs? We're talking Ben Affleck's
back

IS ***** GIVING AUTHORITARIANISM A BAD NAME?

Track 17: "Harvest Moon" by Neil Young. Focus on the part where he sings
about dreaming the night away. Imparting the listener to come closer. I
have something I want to say, the throat clearing of tradition. Is everyone
under the impression that this is a romantic song? It's such a perennial
wedding jam but isn't it about remembering someone who died or at least
broke up with you? "I loved <past tense> you with all my heart"?

I'm on one of those Twitter
chains (brace yourself for some annoying,
thoroughly modern love-in-the-time-of-apps bullcrap)
something like "Describe Yourself in an Album Cover,"
someone tags me and ten
people
and Leo
which is the first time I've seen his
screenname since before we broke
up and there's something like a thrill
that also feels arthritic
and like nostalgia
like a creepy nostalgia
the way a harpsichord sounds
but also like a safety of loving someone without condition
until the condition comes
by which I mean DEEPLY CONFUSING

Track 18: "Crazy" by Seal. Now this song *is* bombast. But it's true. You
have to try. You're not getting a thing by cooping up yr actions, Teebs.
Word to the thighs. Also is this or is this not about an elder doing drugs
for the first time asking for a friend

but then Leo likes my
response and a few other of my tweets
and then we're watching each other's Instagram stories
again and he winds up in my DMs
making one of his dumb puns
about that really popular gay
movie and then we're lobbing
them back and forth almost like a sports metaphor
if I didn't find sports metaphors so disgusting
and it's friendly

but not flirty
not suggestive
but suggesting something
new
in a way that makes me think of the possibilities of jagged spring

[in three voices, like a braid: Wildflower Field & Radial Plantings]
prairie sage, Salvia azurea;
tall tickseed, Coreopsis tripteris;
willowleaf sunflower, Helianthus salicifolius

I guess this is a dirge
to the future I thought we could have
Not all plants were meant to grow together
in the same microclimate. Some things grow apart instead.

Heat is a vital broker between separate things. Yes, don't let it burn.
But also, don't let it fade.

Recognize attraction without pathologizing each other: We tried.
Everything. Both of us, hard. I'm on the other side of another closed
door but I know what the room looks like and I don't need to be in
there. The train stopped running. Interstate trucking, global air travel,
containerized shipping left the hanging train hanging

Track 19: "Up the Ladder to the Roof" by The Supremes. This must
have stuck in Diana's craw bc this got famous after she left but I
digress. The wonder of being closer to the sky. The heavens. You don't
actually see them that much better being higher tbh I mean if that's
the conceit I would say get out of the city to see heaven much better
but that's too wordy I guess. Shut off the light to see the lights.

And even there, to have engines of appetites in a city in a state in a
nation in a world in a solar system in a galaxy in a universe where
the only constant is change—body roll with the punches and the
punchlines and the *I can't stand the rains*. Yes, our High Line stopped
running, but it didn't go away

We bust
the olives before shaving meat sleeves
from its pit. I can feel the chili seeds
from the backseat
of the maroon Honda in Santa Fe 25 years ago.

The ubiquity of garlic
breath.

I'm obsessed with softening, the going in between.

Dear Leo I mean dear reader
sigh
I still indulge wisps of the thought process
that leads me to cut in front of him in line
in my cow skull mind Bratty flirt getting him rock
hard w/ even the slightest denim swipe against his zip fly
"Fuck," he'd say, growling into my neck.

In the park not far from where we first met, in the seats by the popsicle
stand. Blackberry ones were the best. Mango, second to the best.
Coconut was trash. "I think you want to be with *someone*, so clearly so
deep. It just doesn't feel like you want to be with *me*." Leo looked up
at me full Eeyore face. "I been thinkin the same thing."

You're a shade
You mince the length of the sidewalk with me,
sit where I sit, on the sectional
or on the jet plane
and someday you peel from me like a rind

"Mince" is a criminally underused word iykwim (aityd)

I thought up a joke today about the eclipse, telling the moon to
WERK BINCH SIT ON THAT SUN'S FACE YOU LUNAR SLUT
YAAAAS and got sad I couldn't river next to you and whisper up

FWIW I thought you'd bust
a gut

[in three voices, like a braid: Rail Yards]
Kentucky coffee trees, Gymnocladus dioicus; gim-no-KLA-dus dye-oh-
EYE-kuss
foxglove beardtongue, Penstemon digitalis; pen-STEE-mun didge-ih-
TAY-liss
Queen Anne's lace, Daucus carota; DAW-kus kuh-ROE-tuh

Because you see dear reader, in the garden
dry foliage from the previous year's growth gives its sugars
to the new generation. Helps protect
plants from desiccating and freezing in the winter.
Shelter for birds, hibernating
butterflies, and other insects.

Death cycle interwoven with the spring.

It took time to forget
about who we were together, so we could come back
with intention and not surrender

Jiddy says *that makes sense* across from me at the Echo Park vegan
brunch spot mid sorrel-bowl hoovering. *Your pheromones have to
recalibrate*

Spring is a season of reconciliation, a suture
for the loss of winter and the summer's sweaty
promises. Sparklers
on the beach
It's July 4th and we've said no
to imperialism but yes
to public sex

We drive for hours because it's an excuse to sing
together and I forget other people
are around and we're driving
to the coast and the radio is cranked all the way up
and our inhibitions cranked all the way
down
Our layered associations, our accidental landscape.

I've tended to the garden
of our memories, like a recipe
for feelings. The derelict railroad I see when I close my eyes
grown wild with Queen Anne's lace—

In order to see
what we would become, what we were supposed to be, we
had to abandon
ourselves. We had to go derelict,

go wild. Let the living dynamics
of the world outside us grow over us, separately—
and then recreate our *wilder*ness
with a shimmery *wild*ness

Not constantly recreating our memory

THIS IS WHAT A NUCLEAR STRIKE WOULD LOOK LIKE IN
THE HEART OF MANHATTAN

Joe argues for the blast zone
In Hawaii they planted taro to stay alive

The waves recede and the sand looks alive with critters. Pluck them
out of the ground, out of the spot on your back. You will not bleed out,
I promise. Offer these crawling things up to the sun and let them go.
Feel around for the spot and look inside. See? There's molten golden
hour in there It flows inside you You are in the room with your mother
and father pinned against the wall Hug yourself, the small you, an act
of gold The golden was growing inside you even then See it? The fire
that burns inside you Stand up and hug your mother and father They
are so happy to see you So happy with how you live Scoop up some of
the gold and offer it to them They take the shine and radiate and offer
it to their mothers and their fathers, who offer it to their mothers and
their fathers and so on down the line to the site of the rupture Now the
room of your family glows—the vows you made to stay protected need
to be retaken Clear out the fear of being hurt
and the ancestors step aside.

In *Year of the Dog*, Molly Shannon plays a woman who increasingly
becomes a full-on dog lady, it seems to the detriment of her romantic
life, her friendships and her family. But in her final monologue voice
over on the way to an animal rights protest she says, "there are . . . so

many things to love. The love for a husband or a wife. A boyfriend, a girlfriend. The love for children, the love for yourself, and even material things. This is *my* love, it is *mine* and it fills me and it defines me and it compels me on."

I'm back home high
on a roof
top
with Leo on one of those magical

MILITARY BASES TO START BUILDING TENTS TO HOUSE
MIGRANT FAMILIES

"I can't wait until yr a high school English teacher with an Audre
Lorde construction paper quote on the wall" He passes me the spliff
"Leo, are we just Sally Bowlesing this shit right now?"

It's one of those magical
spring early sherbet skies where the city warps forward
into its summer self before dipping
back
down
into the lows tomorrow

and I'm recounting the dude
at the governors corner guest cottages
who hocked spit on me balls deep
before I kicked him out kicking and screaming
and Leo turns to me half lidded saying, "this should have been the
plot of the Lion King"

Iron rattling rattles our laughing as we both turn toward the rattling
ladder hoops and Wilkes pops her head up. She jaunts over to us

on the blue flowered bedsheet spread out with chips and guac and
cucumber sandwiches and pulls tall cans of rosé out of her tote bag,
handing us each one. "You better kick with that shit." She reaches out
to me and I hand her the spliff.

We're listening
to this Neil deGrasse Tyson podcast where they talk
about the God Gene something cellular that makes us look up
and beyond and wonder at our creator
and Stephen Hawking talks
religion and science, saying they both articulate
the nature of who
we are, where we came from and why
and that though science produces more consistent
results, people will always choose religion
because it makes them feel less

alone

a   lone

and the debate turns to whether we're alone in the cosmos and by
then
the edible is hitting like a gif of Daffy Duck in pjs pounding his butt
against a wall so I'm thinking about the words "cosmos" and "cosmetic"
derivative of the Greek *kósmos* meaning order, arrangement
and the guest hopes we're alone because if not? If we encounter
another alien civilization they would likely be faaaaaaaar
more technologically advanced than us, "and look," she says
"how that worked out for the Native Americans"

Imagine you are a circuit.

Imagine whirring electricity.

Imagine being fed, and feeding.

Imagine getting what you need.

Imagine the fire inside you.

Imagine heat.

I don't have much of anything figured out, but I do know to be
indigenous is not to be a miracle of circumstance but to be the golden
light of relentless cunning.

Leo: Right now is forever, for now
he says exhaling & that thought will be deep for approximately three
more hours.
Me: Honestly, I can't stare into the sky for too long without feeling like
I'm about to lose my mind . . . the only living planet in a whole cold
universe.
Wilkes practically stubs out her sub sandwich instead of the smoke.
Wilkes: Again with this shit? Nothing about our evolution strikes me as
predetermined. Come on. I feel with all this exoplanet SETI bullshit
you keep talking about, we're ringing the universe's doorbell with our
Jehovah's Witness pamphlets and lots of societies and worlds and shit are
pretending not to be home. Why would an intelligent society welcome
contact with us? Particularly if they're in any way familiar with our work?
She turns to me, her eyebrows saying, "where's the lie?"
Me: It's not a grief! That we're alone makes me treasure life that much
more. This is our one and only Earth. These are our finite lives. You
are my friends. The idea of us being alone makes me want to hold on
to life, hold on to you that much more but not the choking kind.
Wilkes and Leo are silent a few seconds before looking at each other

and snorting laughter.
Leo: Wow, that shit hit you pretty hard huh?
Wilkes: High Teebs is a corny, bold, sensual Teebs
Leo: One time when we were dating—
Tommy: OKAY, this hang out is officially over this is where you pack
in your snacks and get the fuck off of my roof you bullies
Wilkes relents in a way where she really doesn't. Nobody is going
anywhere.

Let go
of the overgrowth, the unhealthy attachment
to attachment
for the sake of attachment
Imagine letting loose
the expectation to keep white
shoes radiation

The grace
of the dusty rocking chair in the mind The crescendo
moves on into the
denouement

We're nearing the base

of the mountain, the end
of the walk and I think
can art also be the God Gene? The art
gene because what is writing
but convening with the perception of a higher power but a Sunday but
a worship
Alone in the presence

All those disgusting people in the Myspace
days with the profile headline MUSIC
IS MY BOYFRIEND

Yes I'm mewing
into the void and yes
I'm completely

alone

Nations are always outlived by their cities

and Yes, there is utility
in this loneliness This is how *I* be *with*
You, dear reader, on the other
side of my words on the other side
of my worship
on the other side of my shiver winter
hearing my prayer Cupped
in covers
like a pair of hands

A communion wafer in my yellow heart

The father the son and the biblical three-way

Smith & Wesson math lesson XO message in a bottle of wild turkey

As their eyes
were watching
Beyoncé